BUILDING

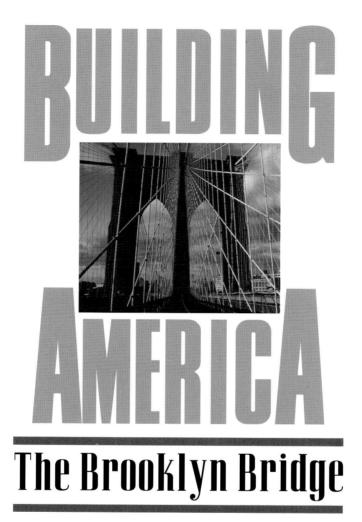

AMERICA

The Brooklyn Bridge

Elaine Pascoe

A BLACKBIRCH PRESS BOOK

WOODBRIDGE, CONNECTICUT

Published by Blackbirch Press, Inc.
260 Amity Road
Woodbridge, CT 06525
web site: http://www.blackbirch.com
e-mail: staff@blackbirch.com

Printed in the Hong Kong

10 9 8 7 6 5 4 3 2 1

Editorial Director: Bruce Glassman
Editorial Assistant: Jenifer Corr Morse

Photo Credits

Cover: ©PhotoDisc; pages 4, 7, 16 (middle & bottom), 28, 29, 41, 42: ©PhotoDisc; pages 8, 9, 18, 19, 27, 33, 35 (right), 39, 40: ©New York Public Library—Astor, Lenox, and Tilden Foundations; page 10: ©New York Historical Society; pages 12, 13, 15, 20, 21, 22, 25, 32 (top), 34, 36, 37: ©Roebling Collection, Rensselaer Polytechnic Institute; pages 4, 28: ©Bruce Glassman; page 16 (top): © Jim McWilliams Photography; page 30: ©Rutgers University; pages 32 (bottom), 35 (left): ©Brooklyn Public Library—Brooklyn Collection; page 38: ©The Museum of the City of New York.

Library of Congress Cataloging-in-Publication Data
Pascoe, Elaine.
    The Brooklyn Bridge / Elaine Pascoe.
        p. cm.—(Building America)
    Includes bibliographical references and index.
    Summary: A history of the Brooklyn Bridge with an emphasis on the basic architecture, engineering, and mechanical procedures of construction.
    ISBN 1-56711-173-4 (lib.bdg.)
    1. Brooklyn Bridge (New York, N.Y.)—Juvenile literature. [1. Brooklyn Bridge (New York N.Y.)] I. Title. II. Series.
TG25.N53 p37 1999   98–46096
624'.5'09747—dc21   CIP
                                                                          AC

Table of Contents

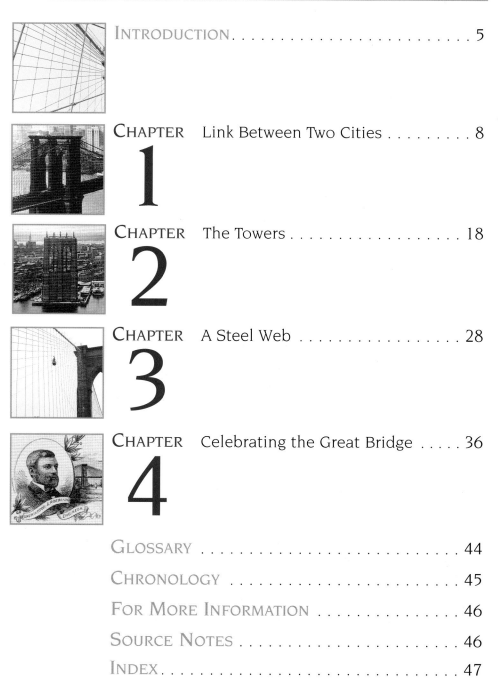

Introduction

On May 24, 1883, the people of Manhattan and Brooklyn gathered to celebrate the creation of a link between their two cities—the newly completed Brooklyn Bridge, spanning the East River. Crowds packed the bridge's deck and spilled over for blocks on each shore awaiting the official dedication ceremony. Even the river was crowded—steamboats and sailing vessels jockeyed for position near the bridge, ringing their bells and tooting their horns.

Those in the crowd who managed to get within hearing distance listened as speaker after speaker pronounced the bridge an engineering marvel. It was the equal of the pyramids of ancient Egypt, one official declared. It was, said another, "the crowning glory of an age memorable for great industrial achievements."

Manhattan and Brooklyn had good reason to be proud of their new bridge. It was the longest suspension bridge in the world, and the first to use steel rather than iron cable. Its twin stone towers were taller than any building in either city, except the spire of New York's Trinity Church. But all this glory came with a price. The bridge had taken 14 years to build, and cost $15 million. More than 20 people—including the bridge's designer—had died during construction.

Since 1883 many longer bridges have been built. The stone towers today are dwarfed by surrounding buildings. But the Brooklyn Bridge remains unique, and its breathtaking design continues to inspire artists, writers, and the thousands of people who cross it every day.

The Manhattan skyline provides a dramatic backdrop for the bridge's nighttime profile.

Link Between Two Cities

The idea of a bridge between Brooklyn and New York City was first proposed in 1802, in a petition to the New York State legislature. At that time, New York City was a bustling port on Manhattan Island, while Brooklyn was a quiet farming village on Long Island. New York City was a market for Brooklyn's farm produce, and farmers wanted to reach it. But spanning the swirling waters of the East River was beyond the bridge-building skills of the day.

One of the first actual designs for an East River bridge was put forward in 1811 by Thomas Pope, a carpenter and self-described architect. His plan called for an enormous wooden arch that would soar more

Opposite:
The Brooklyn Bridge connected a rural farming area with a bustling big city.

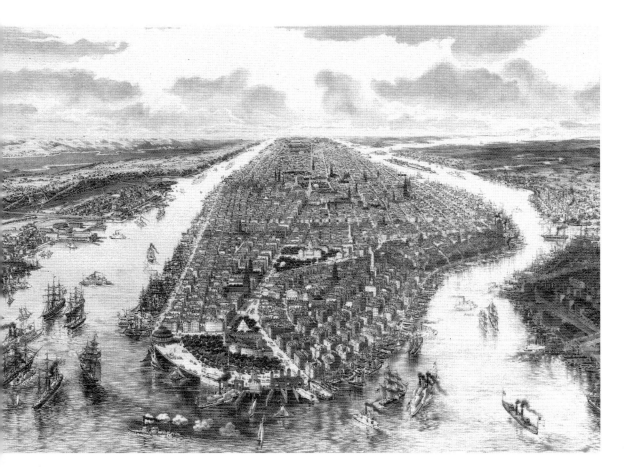

Manhattan Island in 1866. Before the bridge, ferries were needed for travel between Manhattan and Brooklyn.

than 200 feet above the river. Few people shared his confidence that such a bridge could be built, however, and the proposal got a poor reception. In the 1830s, a plan to build a tunnel met with no better success. People continued to cross the river the way they always had—by boat.

By the mid-1800s, steam-powered ferries linked Manhattan and Brooklyn. Steam was a great improvement over the oars and sails that powered earlier boats, and the faster, more reliable new ferries helped Brooklyn grow. Brooklyn became home to new businesses that manufactured everything from buggy whips to tinware. Many people who worked in New York City chose to live on the quieter, eastern side of the river. Brooklyn's population increased from 8,000 early in the century to about 300,000 in 1865, making it America's third-largest city. The ferry boats plied the East River day and night, carrying more than 40 million passengers a year.

But crossing the great river by ferry was often inconvenient—and sometimes dangerous. Fog, ice, and storms could delay the crossing by half a day or more. During the winter of 1866-67, the river was often blocked with so much ice that it could only be crossed on foot. On some days, travelers from Albany—150 miles to the north—reached Manhattan faster than those from Brooklyn. Moreover, the ferry boats were crowded, and traffic on the river was heavier each year. Accidents were inevitable. In 1868, two ferries collided, killing a boy and injuring 20 other people.

All these problems helped keep the idea of a bridge alive. And meanwhile, technology was advancing. By the 1860s, a bridge across the East River no longer seemed impossible to build.

The Engineer

One of those who dreamed of building the bridge was John A. Roebling, a German engineer who had immigrated to the United States. According to one story, Roebling envisioned the Brooklyn Bridge while waiting to make a ferry crossing on the ice-clogged East River in 1852. Whether that story is true or not, as early as 1856 he was in contact with various people who were promoting the idea of an East River bridge.

The bridge site that most appealed to Roebling crossed the East River not to Brooklyn but to Long

JOHN A. ROEBLING

The Brooklyn Bridge was just one of the dreams John Roebling turned into reality during his life. A different dream—the dream of freedom and opportunity—brought him to the United States from Germany, where he was born in 1806. Roebling studied engineering at the University of Berlin and then emigrated in 1831, with a brother and a small group of friends. They were headed for the open spaces of the West, but their money ran out near Pittsburgh, Pennsylvania. They stopped there and founded a small farming community that became known as Saxonburg.

Within a few years, the community prospered—and Roebling grew bored with farming. He took a job as an engineer on a canal-building project in western Pennsylvania. At that job, he got the idea to produce America's first wire rope. Cables woven of iron wire, he realized, would be thinner and stronger, and last longer, than the thick hemp ropes being used for heavy towing and hauling. He began to experiment at his farm in Saxonburg. In 1841 he sold his first wire rope for use in the Pennsylvania canal project.

From that invention, it was a short step to adapt the rope for building suspension bridges. Roebling's first suspension design, built in 1844, was for an aqueduct that would carry the canal over the Allegheny River. This aqueduct was like a bridge, but it had a channel for water instead of a roadway for passengers. In 1847, he built a suspension bridge across the Monongahela River in Pittsburgh. Three years later, he took over a project to build a bridge over the Niagara Gorge in New York State. When the first loaded freight train rolled across the 821-foot span, Roebling's reputation was made.

The Roebling wire-rope business grew rapidly. In 1849 he moved with his family to Trenton, New Jersey, and opened a factory. He was constantly working on improvements to his wire

Island City, in Queens. There, the crossing could be made with two modest bridges—one from Manhattan to Blackwell's (now Roosevelt) Island, and one from Blackwell's to Long Island. Roebling wasn't able to get the project off the ground, however, and

rope, including the use of steel wire in place of iron. In 1857 he began work on a suspension bridge over the Ohio River in Cincinnati. It took ten years to build. When completed, it had a main span of 1,057 feet—a record at the time.

In person, Roebling frequently seemed quiet and disinterested. But, beneath that exterior, was a quirky personality. He believed in spiritualism—the idea that living people can communicate with the spirits of the dead at gatherings called séances. He also believed that water could cure all illnesses. He drank large quantities of it and took cold baths daily. As odd as these ideas might have seemed to others, few people doubted his skills as an engineer.

John Roebling's company produced America's first wire rope.

the Queensboro Bridge was eventually built at the site. In 1857 Roebling wrote to the industrialist Abram Hewitt, suggesting a bridge to Brooklyn instead. Hewitt began to promote the idea, and it gained the support of powerful politicians on both sides of the river. With their backing, the plan for the Great East River Bridge was approved by the New York State legislature in 1867.

A private company, the New York Bridge Company, was formed to undertake the construction, with the understanding that Manhattan and Brooklyn would be able to buy the completed bridge at cost. That cost was estimated at $7 million, plus the cost of land for the approach ramps on each shore. John Roebling was named chief engineer.

The Design

An experienced bridge-builder, Roebling knew that only a suspension bridge would be strong enough to span the East River. But the requirements for such a bridge were daunting. The bridge would stretch more than 3,000 feet from shore to shore, not including approach ramps. It would have to be high enough to allow tall-masted ships to pass under, and strong enough to withstand the winds that whipped along the river during storms.

Roebling's design called for two massive stone support towers, over 276 feet tall and weighing 67,850 tons. They would be set deep into the river bottom. Thick cables of steel wire rope would loop over the towers from stone anchorages on shore. Each anchorage would stand seven stories tall and cover most of a city block—larger than most buildings in New York at the time.

Between the towers, the cables would support a center span of nearly 1,600 feet—half again as long as the longest suspension span built to date. The span would be as high as 130 feet above the water.

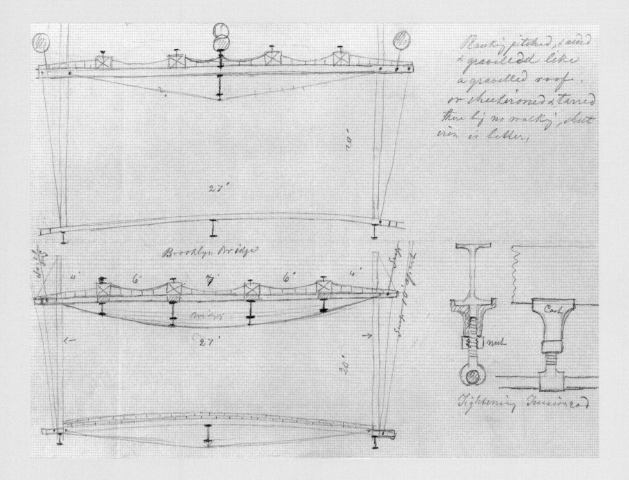

Heavy trusses and stay cables would keep it from twisting in the wind. It would be a "great avenue" between Brooklyn and Manhattan, Roebling said, wide enough for two carriage lanes and two cable-car lines. Above the main roadway, an elevated boardwalk would allow pedestrians to stroll across the bridge and admire views that stretched across Manhattan and south to New Jersey.

It was a bold plan, and there were plenty of people who said the bridge could never be built.

From his earliest sketches, Roebling had always envisioned a suspension design for the Brooklyn Bridge.

HIGH SUSPENSE

A *stone arch bridge*.

When John Roebling drew his plans for the Brooklyn Bridge, large suspension bridges were still a new and daring concept. Most bridges were flat spans that rested on supports and trestles, or arches that rose from foundations at each end. In a suspension bridge, support comes from above. Cables pass over two support towers and are firmly anchored on each shore. Vertical suspender cables hang from the main cables and hold up the bridge roadway, or deck.

Small suspension foot bridges were made in early times using rope and, later, metal chain for the cables. It wasn't possible to build big suspension bridges until woven iron and steel cables were developed in the 1840s. Wire rope cables were strong enough to hold up a heavy deck with a long span—long enough to cross wide rivers and deep chasms.

Engineers had to solve other problems, however. A bridge must be strong enough to support its own weight and the weight of the traffic it carries. It must also stand up to wind and weather. A suspension bridge built in 1849 over the Ohio River near Wheeling, West Virginia, collapsed five years later when wind set the span swaying. The bridge deck picked up momentum, swinging back and forth like a pendulum until the cables gave way. That catastrophe taught engineers to stiffen a bridge deck with solid trusses, to reduce sway.

Today's suspension bridges are far larger than early ones. The world's longest suspension bridge is the Akashi Kaikyo Bridge in Japan. This structure, which opened in 1998, crosses a strait between the city of Kobe and Awaji Island. It is 12,906 feet long, with a center span of 6,570 feet—more than four times longer than the center span of the Brooklyn Bridge.

Other non-suspension designs:
Concrete floating bridge (below),
Cantilever bridge (bottom).

Roebling, however, was confident. "As a work of art, and a successful specimen of advanced bridge engineering, this structure will forever testify to the energy, enterprise, and wealth of that community which shall secure its erection," he wrote.

To set his plan in motion, he set about choosing sites for the anchorages at each end of the bridge. On the Manhattan side, he picked a location near City Hall. The anchorage there would cover the site on Cherry Street where George Washington had lived from 1789 to 1790, when New York City was the capital of the United States. The approach ramp would start farther west, at Chatham Street. On the Brooklyn side, Roebling chose a site just below Brooklyn Heights, an elegant neighborhood overlooking the city.

Triumph & Tragedy

In 1869 the bridge proposal cleared its last hurdle, winning approval from the federal government. Construction could begin at last. But John Roebling did not live to see it. On June 28, 1869, he was at the Fulton Street ferry slip in Brooklyn, helping to fix the precise location for the Brooklyn support tower. He was standing at the edge of the wharf when an incoming ferry bumped against the structure. Roebling's foot was caught and crushed between some pilings. The injury was serious—his toes had to be amputated. He then developed tetanus, an infection for which there was no antitoxin. He died on July 22.

The job of building the East River Bridge, as it was known, fell to his son Washington Roebling. He was 32, and the bridge would consume the next 14 years of his life.

2

The Towers

Washington Roebling graduated from Rensselaer Polytechnic Institute with a degree in civil engineering. He had worked alongside his father on earlier projects and had helped prepare the plans for this one. He had also traveled to Europe to learn more about a construction device that would be central to the building of the Brooklyn Bridge. That device was the pneumatic caisson (large wooden platform), which would be used to anchor the huge support towers beneath the riverbed.

The problem was that the river bottom was covered with thick layers of mud, silt, and loose stones. Such soft material could never support the towers.

Opposite:
The Manhattan tower, under construction between 1870–1875.

19

After the death of his father, Washington Roebling headed up the massive bridge project.

It had to be removed, so that the towers could rest on firm ground or bedrock. Support platforms called caissons would help to provide solid footing by resting on the river bottom. Roebling described the caissons as giant diving bells. Each was an enormous wooden box, watertight on the top and sides, but open on the bottom. The stone towers would be built on the tops of the caissons, which would eventually be made of solid concrete and were big enough to comfortably fit six tennis courts. As stone was added, the caissons would be pushed into the riverbed. At the same time, compressed air would be pumped into the caisson, to keep water out and allow workers inside to dig out the gravel and boulders at the bottom of the river.

Caissons had been used for underwater construction before. But no one had built caissons as large as the ones that would be needed for the Brooklyn Bridge, or tried to sink them as deep. And no one could say if the plan would work.

Under the River

The caissons were built at a shipyard upriver and launched into the water like ships. They were constructed of water-resistant pitch pine, with tops 15 feet thick to support the stone that would be piled on them. Their walls tapered to an iron-covered shoe that would dig into the riverbed. The Brooklyn caisson was launched first and floated into position in May, 1870. At first, it bobbed up and down with the tides. But by late June, enough stone had been laid on top of the box to keep it firmly anchored.

INSIDE THE CAISSON

A trip into one of the Brooklyn Bridge caissons was something no one ever forgot. Workers entered by stepping down through a hatch into an air lock. The hatch was closed, and compressed air was pumped into the lock until its pressure was equal to that inside the caisson below. Then a second hatch at the bottom of the air lock opened, and the workers climbed down into the caisson.

The scene that greeted them was nightmarish. Heavy bulkheads divided the caisson into six sections. Eerie, blue-white light from calcium lamps (the same "limelights" then used in theaters) bathed the sections where men were at work. Other sections were cloaked in murky darkness. The air was heavy, hot, and damp. Mud coated everything, and pools of mud and water covered the bottom. Workers stripped to the waist, wore rubber boots, and walked around on raised planks.

The compressed air that filled the interior had strange effects on those who entered. E. F. Farrington, the master mechanic on the job, described it this way: "There was a confused sensation in the head, like 'the rush of many waters.' The pulse was at first accelerated, then sometimes fell below normal. The voice sounded faint and unnatural, and it became a great effort to speak." With flaming lights and deep shadows and the racket of hammers, drills, and chains, Farrington said, the caisson was like "a vision of hell."

This original sketch by Roebling shows his design for an iron caisson that went from 60 x 138 feet at the top to 70 x 148 feet at the bottom.

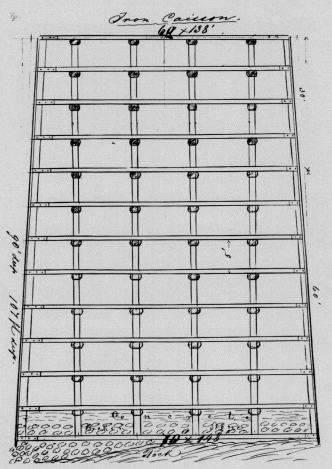

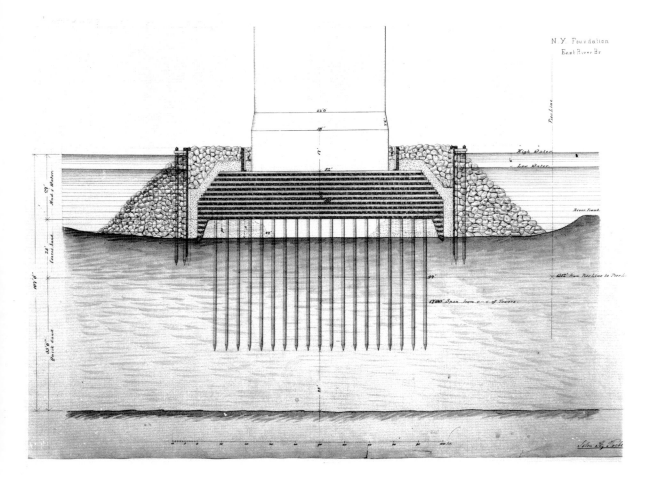

N.Y. Foundation
East River Br

Roebling's sketch shows the foundation design. The plan notes the conditions: 27 feet of mud and water; 25 feet of coarse sand; 55 feet of quick sand.

Inside the caisson, progress was slow. Workers hacked away at boulders with steel bars and sledgehammers, breaking them up so they could be removed and would not block the caisson's descent. It was grueling, time-consuming work. As the caisson sank deeper and encountered many larger boulders, Roebling decided to start blasting them apart. There was great concern that blasting might damage the caisson or harm workers, but that didn't happen.

The work went on day and night, stopping only on Sundays. Most of the workers were immigrants—Irish, German, and Italian. Immigrants were arriving in New York in great numbers during the 1870s, and many were desperate to find work. Caisson laborers earned $2 a day to start, a decent wage at the time. But turnover was high, because many could not tolerate the work for long. Conditions in the caisson were terrible—the air was dank, and the temperature never fell below 80 degrees Fahrenheit. In addition, the work was quite dangerous. Workers knew that if the caisson failed, they would likely be crushed by its enormous weight or drowned by inrushing water.

Fears increased in December 1870, when workers discovered that fire was smoldering deep in the roof timbers of the Brooklyn caisson. To put it out, they had to stop work and flood the structure. After two days, the water was pumped out, and work resumed. The caisson had only 2 more feet to go before it reached its final depth, 44 feet 6 inches below the riverbed. But it took three months to repair the damage done to the roof and make it strong again. Then, in March 1871, the entire structure was filled with concrete.

A Mysterious Threat

In May 1871 the Manhattan caisson was launched. Roebling made it even larger and stronger than the Brooklyn caisson because he figured it would have to go deeper to reach solid ground. He was right—but he didn't realize how dangerous the descent would be.

Workers first had to dig through a layer of clay silt blackened by sewage, which made the inside of the caisson reek. Below that they found sand and gravel, with very few boulders. The work went fast. In a month, the caisson had burrowed 45 feet into the riverbed, and it kept going down. Now, besides unpleasant working conditions and the fear that the caisson might fail, workers had to contend with another danger: A mysterious ailment called caisson disease, or "the bends."

Workers who emerged from the caisson would sometimes double over in pain, pass out, or be unable to move, and no one knew why. Today this condition is known to be brought on by changes in surrounding air pressure. The deeper one goes under water, the higher the pressure. High pressure (like that inside the caisson) causes nitrogen gas to dissolve in the blood. A sudden return to normal air pressure causes the gas to come out of solution and form bubbles in the bloodstream. The bubbles block blood flow and damage body tissues. The problem can be prevented, as deep-sea divers now know, by returning to normal pressure slowly. But in 1872, doctors didn't know how to treat the terrible symptoms of caisson disease. They prescribed special diets, rest, and shortened work shifts.

Caisson disease was a minor problem for workers on the Brooklyn caisson. It became a serious problem on the Manhattan caisson, which went much deeper. As depth increased, the air pressure required inside the caisson also increased. So did the number and severity of cases of caisson disease. Most of the attacks lasted several hours. Roebling himself suffered several attacks. Then, in April 1872, two men actually died.

Opposite: Work on the Manhattan-side foundation progressed from above ground, around 1869.

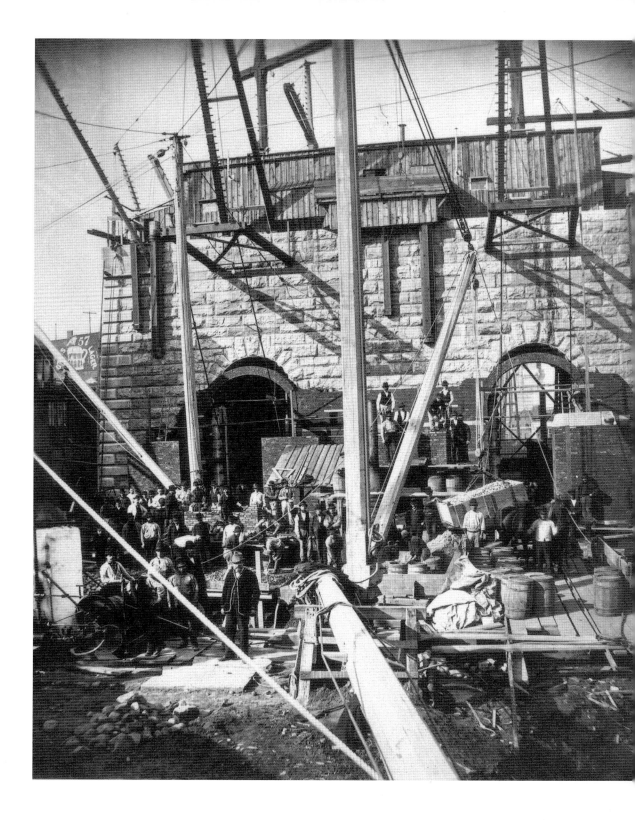

The caisson was now more than 70 feet down. How much farther would it have to go to reach bedrock? Roebling ordered soundings to be taken. They showed that the bedrock below the caisson was jagged and uneven. It would have to be blasted level to make a foundation, which meant months of work and possibly more lives lost. In May, when a third worker died of the bends, Roebling chose to stop the descent at 78 feet 6 inches. The cement-filled caisson would rest on fine, packed sand.

Not long after that, Roebling suffered another attack of the bends. He collapsed and was rushed home to Brooklyn, near death. He was back at work a few days later, but the painful attacks recurred. Work on the bridge towers continued until winter, but Roebling grew weaker. Even the simple act of issuing instructions to his assistants tired him, and he relied more and more on his wife, Emily, to relay his wishes. When the work resumed in the spring of 1873, Roebling requested a leave of absence. He began to fear that, like his father, he would not live to see the bridge completed.

Washington and Emily Roebling left for Europe, hoping that rest and treatment there would restore his health. Meanwhile, the towers continued to rise according to the plans he left behind. Granite blocks were ferried out to the construction site, hoisted one by one, and guided into position. On top, as many as 80 men might be working at one time. A stiff wind blew, chilling workers to the bone. And tower work had its own dangers. Three men died as a result of falls from the tower tops, and several others were crushed by falling stone or killed in other accidents.

Despite these tragedies, work on the towers continued. At 119 feet, the height of the bridge deck, the solid stone opened into soaring arches for the roadway. Then the towers continued to rise up for another 157 feet. The Brooklyn tower was finished in June 1875, and the Manhattan tower in July 1876. By August, it was time to join them with wire.

The towers began to take shape by 1873.

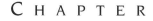

A Steel Web

Washington Roebling returned to Brooklyn late in 1873. He and Emily purchased a house in Brooklyn Heights, with views overlooking the bridge. But they did not stay long. Roebling's health had not improved, and his problem was no longer described as caisson disease, but instead as a "nervous disorder." He was weak, and his eyesight was failing. He suffered from violent headaches and joint and stomach pains. Doctors suggested he get out of the city, so he and Emily went to Trenton, where the family wire-rope business was still thriving.

Even from Trenton, however, Roebling continued to supervise every detail of the bridge, right down to

Opposite:
The huge steel
webs that help
to support the
roadway are one
of the Brooklyn
Bridge's most
unique features.

29

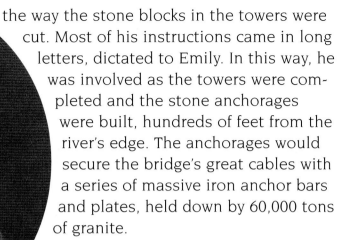

Emily Roebling played an important role in helping her husband finish the bridge.

the way the stone blocks in the towers were cut. Most of his instructions came in long letters, dictated to Emily. In this way, he was involved as the towers were completed and the stone anchorages were built, hundreds of feet from the river's edge. The anchorages would secure the bridge's great cables with a series of massive iron anchor bars and plates, held down by 60,000 tons of granite.

By the summer of 1876, with his health starting to improve, Roebling began to make plans to return to Brooklyn. The work of stretching cables across the towers was about to begin, and he wanted to be there.

Wire Ropes

The first two wire ropes were strung across the river on August 14, 1876. Master mechanic E. F. Farrington directed the operation. First, the rope ends were hauled to the top of the Brooklyn tower, passed through a set of pulleys, and let down the other side. Then they were attached to the stern of a scow, which was pushed by tugboats to the Manhattan tower. Once again the ropes were hauled up and over, and then hauled 900 feet inland to the Manhattan anchorage. At last, the two cities were joined by a slender band of steel!

These first cables were just the working ropes. They were joined in a continuous loop that was turned by engines on the ground. Riding in a boatswain's chair—little more than a board seat,

Boss Tweed and the Brooklyn Bridge

In 1871, the Brooklyn Bridge was caught up in one of the greatest scandals of the day—the fall of William Marcy "Boss" Tweed. In the late 1800s, Boss Tweed controlled the New York City Democratic organization called Tammany Hall, and that gave him enormous power in the city. He and his cohorts—the Tweed Ring—used that power to embezzle money from the city treasury. They put their friends on the city payroll and took bribes.

Some of Tweed's favorite money-making schemes involved kickbacks. Area contractors were encouraged to overbill for city work. They were paid the full amount and quietly returned the overage to the Tweed Ring. Because of this practice, a new city courthouse, started in 1868 with an estimated cost of $500,000, had cost $8 million by 1871—and still wasn't finished.

Tweed was a major shareholder in the Brooklyn Bridge Company. He also held a seat on its Executive Committee. He expected to profit from this huge construction project, through patronage jobs and outright bribery, embezzlement, and kickbacks. Other powerful politicians also had a vested interest in the project and expected to gain from it. But late in 1871, newspapers got wind of Tweed's courthouse scheme and other misdeeds. They printed stories exposing the fraud and those who were responsible. Outraged New Yorkers mounted a campaign against the Tweed Ring, and most of Tweed's people were voted out of office. Tweed himself was arrested.

Tweed's fall, it seemed, came just in time to save the bridge from the sort of fraud that had brought disaster to the courthouse project. Abram Hewitt, the industrialist and reformer who had been instrumental in helping John Roebling get his bridge proposal approved, helped lead the forces against Tweed. Hewitt then took Tweed's place on the Bridge Company's executive committee. In 1874, the bridge's charter was changed, making the "New York and Brooklyn Bridge" a public work, owned by the two cities. Investors were paid off, and the bridge company was dissolved.

attached like a swing to the wires—Farrington became the first person to cross the bridge. More than 10,000 people watched him ride over successfully and cheered. In the weeks that followed, other working ropes were strung. Then the work of making the great cables began.

Top: *A pulley system guides the steel cables.*
Above: *E.F. Farrington was the first person to cross the bridge, in 1876.*

Each of the 4 main cables would eventually contain more than 3,500 miles of wire—enough wire to stretch across the Atlantic Ocean. The wire ropes were spun across the river individually, and then workers went aloft and lashed them into cables nearly 16 inches thick. Many of the men were former sailors, accustomed to working in ships' rigging. Watching these skillful workers became a favorite pastime for people on the ground. But it was dangerous work. In one of the worst accidents, two men were killed when a strand broke loose at the Manhattan anchorage.

When the main cables were completed, hundreds of vertical cables were suspended from them. Steel beams were attached to the suspenders to form the road deck—the largest steel structure yet built. Then diagonal stay cables were added, fanning out from the tops of the towers to the deck. Their job was to add stability, but they also added beauty. Together, the cables formed an elegant, weblike pattern.

The End in Sight

In all, stretching the cables and building the roadway took more than six years. For much of this time, Washington Roebling supervised the work from his house in Brooklyn. He was never again seen at the site. But he could see everything, looking out his back window through a telescope. Emily Roebling made daily visits to the bridge, carrying his instructions and bringing back reports. She became very knowledgeable about the construction methods and was admired and respected by the foremen and assistant engineers.

By early December 1881, suspenders and steel beams were in place from tower to tower. A temporary plank walkway was laid down. Emily Roebling, with a group of the bridge's trustees and reporters, led the first walk across the bridge. But it wasn't until the spring of 1883 that the actual roadway was in and the approaches to the bridge were completed. The approaches were made up of nine different bridges over the waterfronts of Brooklyn and Manhattan. A total of $3.8 million had been spent to buy the land they covered.

Top: Most of the heavy top cable was strung by 1876.
Above: By 1879, a catwalk enabled workers to cross back and forth.

NON-ROEBLING CABLE

This was the first time steel wire was used for a bridge, and, from the beginning, everyone assumed that the Roebling wireworks would supply it. Washington Roebling even gave up his holdings in the family firm, so the company could bid on the project without seeming to have an advantage. But the contract went to another bidder. In 1877, as work on the cables progressed, that contractor was found to have supplied substandard wire. Roebling was outraged. The cables, however, were still designed to be more than six times stronger than they needed to be.

Spools of thin wire are braided together to create heavy bridge cables. These spools are being braided at the Roebling Company in New Jersey.

Left: *Members of the design and construction team gather on the Brooklyn anchorage, October 1878.* Above: *The bridge in 1880. Stonework and cables are still under construction.*

In May, Emily Roebling stepped into a carriage in Brooklyn and was driven at a snappy trot to Manhattan, becoming the first person to ride across the bridge in a vehicle. She carried a rooster in the carriage—a symbol of victory. Despite the celebrations, finishing touches were still being made to the structure. The rail cars (which replaced the cable cars called for in the original design) weren't ready to run. Electric lights—which had been developed while the bridge was being built—were now being installed. For the most part, however, the main work on the bridge was finally over.

The Trustees of the
New York and Brooklyn Bridge

request the honor of the presence of

Mr. and Mrs. Joseph A. Cottier Jr.
at the

Opening Ceremonies

to take place on Thursday, May twenty fourth at two o'clock, P.M.

Committees.

_____ Henry W. Slocum _ Jenkins Van Schaick

_____ Otto Witte

_____ Brooklyn

_____ of New York.

_____ Roebling

The East River Bridge

will be opened to the public

Thursday, May twenty fourth, at 2 o'clock.

Col. & Mrs. Washington A. Roebling

request the honor of your company

after the opening ceremony until

seven o'clock.

110 Columbia Heights,

Brooklyn.

4

Celebrating the Great Bridge

The official opening of the Brooklyn Bridge, on May 24,1883, was an enormous celebration. Some 50,000 people came in from out of town just to attend. Schools and businesses in both cities closed for the day. President Chester A. Arthur was on hand to lead a parade across the new span. Emily Roebling was there in place of her husband, who was stronger than he had been in years, but still not up to the event. Most of the notables, including the president, went to the Roeblings' Brooklyn house for a reception after the ceremony. As night fell, people watched from streets and rooftops as electric lights winked on, outlining the bridge against the dark sky.

Opposite: By 1883, the bridge was finally ready to be opened to the public. These were the official invitations sent out by the bridge's trustees and Washington Roebling himself.

37

A huge nighttime display was the grand finale of the bridge's opening ceremonies.

Then the lights went out, and fireworks exploded high above the bridge—14 tons of fireworks, ending with a 500-rocket grand finale.

During the days that followed, thousands of people paid a penny apiece to walk or drive across the East River's newest star. They were eager to cross what was hailed as the biggest, best bridge in the world—a symbol of progress and promise for the future. As John Roebling had foreseen, the bridge became a major attraction. It was not just a better way to get from Brooklyn to New York. It was the "Eighth Wonder of the World." People came from far and wide to marvel at it. The showman P. T. Barnum arrived in 1884 with a herd of 21 elephants, which he drove across to test the bridge's strength. People from both cities took Sunday promenades on the wooden walkway elevated above the roadbed. From the bridge's great height, they enjoyed fresh breezes and one of the most inspiring views in America.

The bridge had a major effect on the future of Brooklyn and New York. Linked by steel, they grew closer. By the end of the 1800s, Brooklyn was no longer a separate city. It was a borough of New York, and it was growing faster than ever.

Within 50 years of its opening, the Brooklyn Bridge lost its status as the world's longest bridge. But it kept its status as a treasured symbol, especially for the people of Brooklyn. The bridge's elegant blend of stone and steel, its gothic arches, and its threadlike cables made it a favorite subject for artists and photographers. It has figured in countless songs, stories, movies, and plays. Many poems have been written about it. One of the best known, "To Brooklyn Bridge" by Hart Crane, compares the bridge to a harp and an altar.

The bridge in 1898. By the late 1800s, Brooklyn and Manhattan had both experienced great growth as a result of being connected by the bridge.

Painters scale the wire web as they apply the bridge's annual protective coating.

Not everything associated with the Brooklyn Bridge, however, is beautiful. In the bridge's early days, several people tried to jump from it, hoping to win lasting fame. Most were killed. The bridge has also been a popular icon for business. It has been used in advertisements for everything from sewing machines to cowboy boots. It has also appeared on its share of souvenir postcards, paperweights, silver spoons, and T-shirts.

The Brooklyn Bridge was designated a National Historic Landmark in 1964. In 1983, a century after the bridge opened, New York commemorated its 100th anniversary with another great celebration.

Again, there were parades, speeches, and fireworks. Roebling's structure was so solid that the bridge had needed very little repair over the years. The rail lines had been ripped out years earlier, and the bridge was carrying 100,000 cars a day without a wobble. The wooden central walkway, however, was replaced in the early 1980s.

Today, signs along the walkway tell the story of the bridge's construction. They honor the Roeblings and others who built it, and point out the sights that can be viewed from various locations. Among those sights are skyscrapers that loom high over the bridge towers. As tall as they are, none of those buildings can overshadow the bridge's everlasting ability to inspire wonder and admiration in all who see it.

The bridge's long walkway offers visitors some of the world's best views of the Manhattan skyline.

The Brooklyn Bridge remains one of New York's most dramatic and enduring symbols of human engineering.

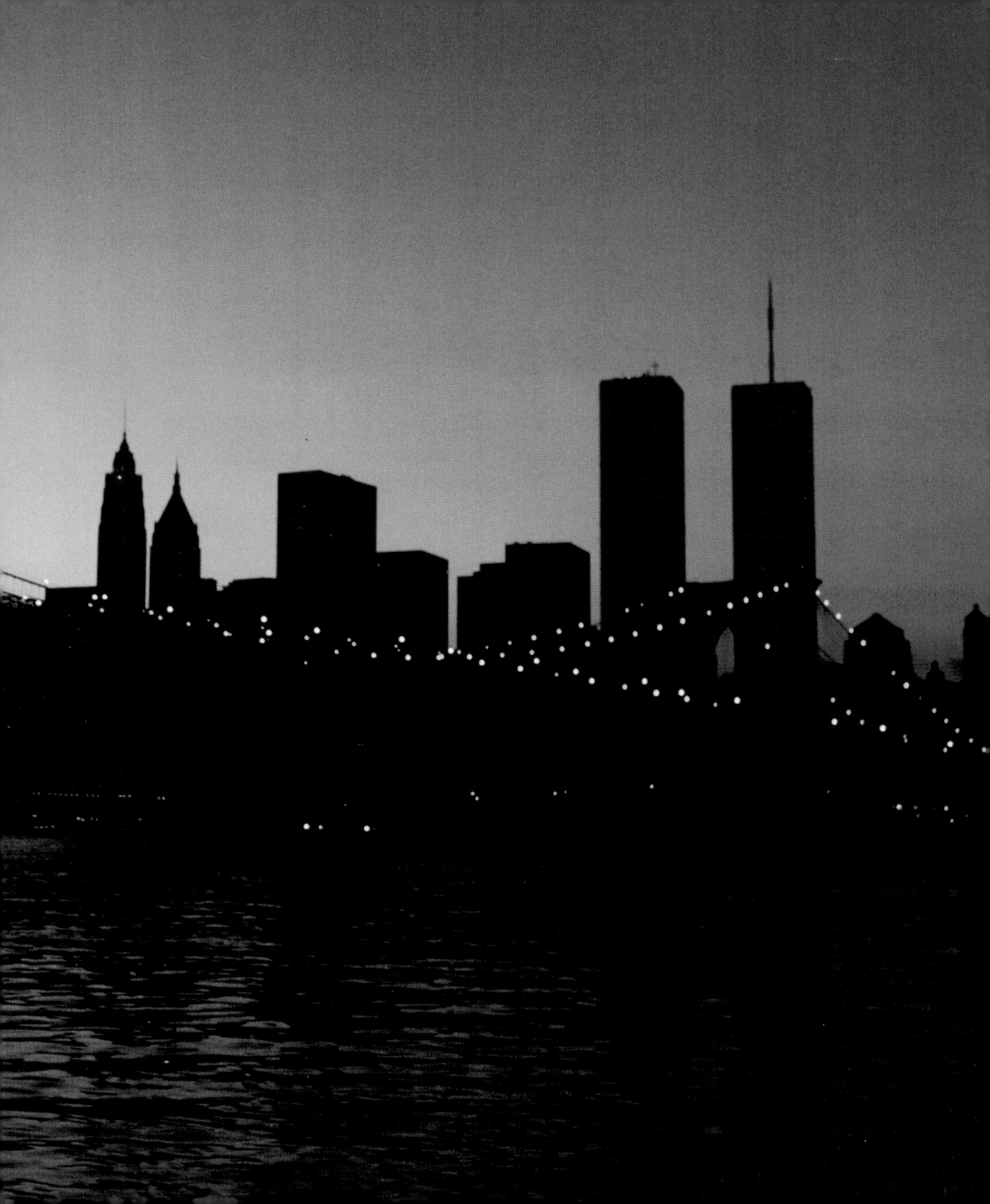

GLOSSARY

air lock An airtight chamber or tunnel that allows passage between two places with different air pressure.

approach A route or means of access to a bridge.

aqueduct A structure that carries a large quantity of flowing water from one place to another.

bedrock The solid rock beneath a loose covering of soil, gravel, or sand.

bulkhead A structure or partition built to shut off water and resist its pressure.

caisson A watertight box used in underwater construction work. Laborers used it as a workroom beneath the river to remove rock and soil from the riverbed.

canal A humanmade waterway for ships or for transporting water to dry areas.

commemorate To remember or mark the importance of by a celebration or ceremony.

embezzle To secretly steal money from a company or person you work for and use it for your own needs.

icon A symbol that represents, or is associated with, a location, person, or time period.

petition A formal written request that is made to an official person or group.

promenade A place for a relaxing walk or ride in a public place; a stroll for amusement. It was a popular social event at the time the bridge was built.

scow A large, flat-bottomed boat with square ends mainly used for transporting material.

seance A meeting to receive communications from the spirits of the dead.

soundings A way to measure the depth of something below the water.

specimen An individual or item considered part of a group, class, or whole, but distinguished by exceptional characteristics.

spire A structure that comes to a point on the top, usually built on a church steeple.

suspension bridge A structure that has its roadway hung and supported from two or more cables, usually passing over towers.

technology The development of products or knowledge in a practical way that makes a job easier and more efficient.

tetanus An infectious disease, acquired by a wound, that causes muscles to tighten uncontrollably, especially in the jaw.

trestles A braced framework of timber, iron, or steel used to carry a bridge over a river, chasm, or other depression in the land.

trusses An assembly of iron beams that secures and strengthens a bridge.

CHRONOLOGY

May 1867 A company is formed to build a bridge across the East River. John Roebling is named chief engineer.

July 1869 John Roebling dies following an accident at the Brooklyn waterfront. His son Washington Roebling takes his place.

1869 The bridge site is surveyed.

1870 Construction of the Brooklyn tower begins.

March 1871 Brooklyn caisson is filled, completing the tower foundation.

May 1871 Manhattan caisson is launched.

July 1872 Manhattan tower foundation is finished.

June 1875 Brooklyn tower is completed.

November 1875 Brooklyn anchorage completed.

July 1876 Manhattan tower and anchorage completed.

August 1876 First wire strung; E. F. Farrington makes first crossing.

October 1878 Main cables are in place.

December 1881 Steel deck structure is completed.

April 1883 Promenade is completed.

May 24, 1883 Bridge officially opens.

FOR MORE INFORMATION

Books

Ardley, Neil. *Bridges*. Ada, OK: Garrett Educational, 1990.

Mann, Elizabeth. *The Brooklyn Bridge*. New York, NY: Mikaya Press, 1996.

Kent, Zachary. *The Story of the Brooklyn Bridge*. Chicago, IL: Children's Press, 1988.

Maze, Stephanie. *I Want to Be an Engineer* (I Want to Be Series). Orlando, FL: Harcourt Brace, 1997.

Oxlade, Chris. *Bridges* (Superstructures). Chatham, NJ: Raintree/Steck Vaughn, 1997.

Spangenburg, Ray. Diane Moser. *The Story of America's Bridges*. New York, NY: Facts on File, 1991.

Videos

A&E Home Video. *Brooklyn Bridge* (Modern Marvels).

PBS Home Video. *Brooklyn Bridge*.

Web Site

Brooklyn Bridge Bookmarks

History of the bridge—www.endex.com/gf/buildings/bbridge/bbridge.html.

SOURCE NOTES

The Great East River Bridge, 1883-1983. New York: Brooklyn Museum, 1983.

Harper's New Monthly Magazine, selected issues. New York: Harper & Brothers, 1870-1883.

McCullough, David. *The Great Bridge: The Epic Story of the Building of the Brooklyn Bridge*. New York: Simon & Schuster, 1972.

Opening Ceremonies of the New York and Brooklyn Bridge, May 24, 1883. Brooklyn, N.Y.: The Brooklyn Eagle Press, 1883.

Sexton, Andrea Wyatt, and Alice Leccese Powers, eds. *The Brooklyn Reader: 30 Writers Celebrate America's Favorite Borough*. New York: Crown, 1994.

Trachtenberg, Alan. *Brooklyn Bridge: Fact and Symbol*. Chicago: University of Chicago Press, 1979.

INDEX